THIS BOOK BELONGS TO

....

LOOK OUT FOR MORE POOP-TASTIC BOOKS IN THIS RANGE:

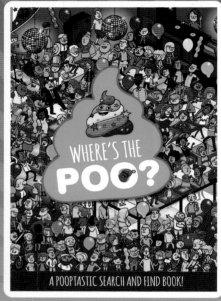

A POOPTASTIC SEARCH AND FIND BOOK!

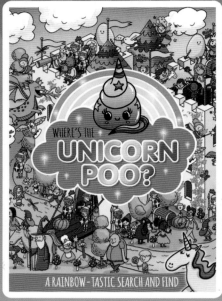

A RAINBOW-TASTIC SEARCH AND FIND

A DINO-TASTIC SEARCH AND FIND

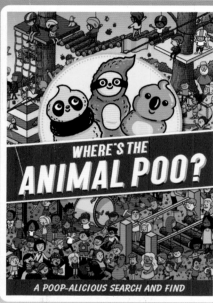

A POOP-ALICIOUS SEARCH AND FIND

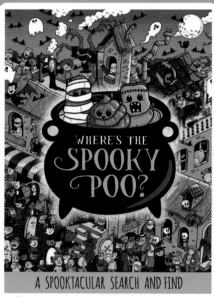

A SPOOKTACULAR SEARCH AND FIND

A POO-PACKED SEARCH AND FIND

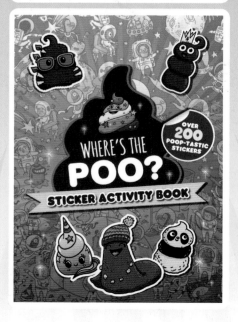

WHERE'S THE SPORTY POO?

ORCHARD

MEET THE POOS

It's game, set and match for the sporty poos as they attempt to bring home as many gold medals as they can. Spot them as they have a go at cycling, diving and lots more fun sports. They're a competitive bunch!

SUPERPOO

is a real thrill-seeker. His favourite sports are skiing and canoeing.

BOBBI

is a talented skateboarder and surprisingly gifted at crazy golf.

QUEENIE

collects gold medals to decorate her U-bend.

DUCKIE

loves making a splash. You can usually find him plunging off a diving board.

ELVIS

likes any sport involving a cool pair of shades.

GOLD MEDAL POO

Gold Medal Poo is the ultimate poo champion. Spot this super special poo in one of the scenes.

POOLSIDE

Bobbi is watching the divers jump, flip and spin into the water, whilst Duckie is dreaming of joining the synchronised swimming team. Can you spot all the poos?

VELO VROOM

The poo friends are getting dizzy watching the racers go round and round the velodrome. Can you find them cheering for their favourite riders?

BALL BONANZA

Uh oh, someone left the storeroom door open. Can you round up the poos before they get buried in all the bouncing balls?

ODD ONE OUT!

Which balls look different to the rest?

PUTTING POOS

Pitch and putt ... with poos! Bobbi's ball is stuck in the windmill but Queenie is having better luck – she just got a hole in one!

ON YOUR MARKS

It's time to spot the sporty poos at the athletics track. Watch out for the runners crossing the finish line.

STINKY WICKET

Do you know which sport can be played with these objects? First identify the sport and then find the poos hiding.

ODD ONE OUT!

Which ball and bat don't match the others?

SPEED SEEKERS

It's noisy and dusty down at the racetrack. Elvis wants to test drive a go-kart. Remember to wear a helmet, Elvis!

IT'S SNOW JOKE

The skiers and snowboarders are having fun on the slopes, gliding across the snow. Watch out for flying snowballs!

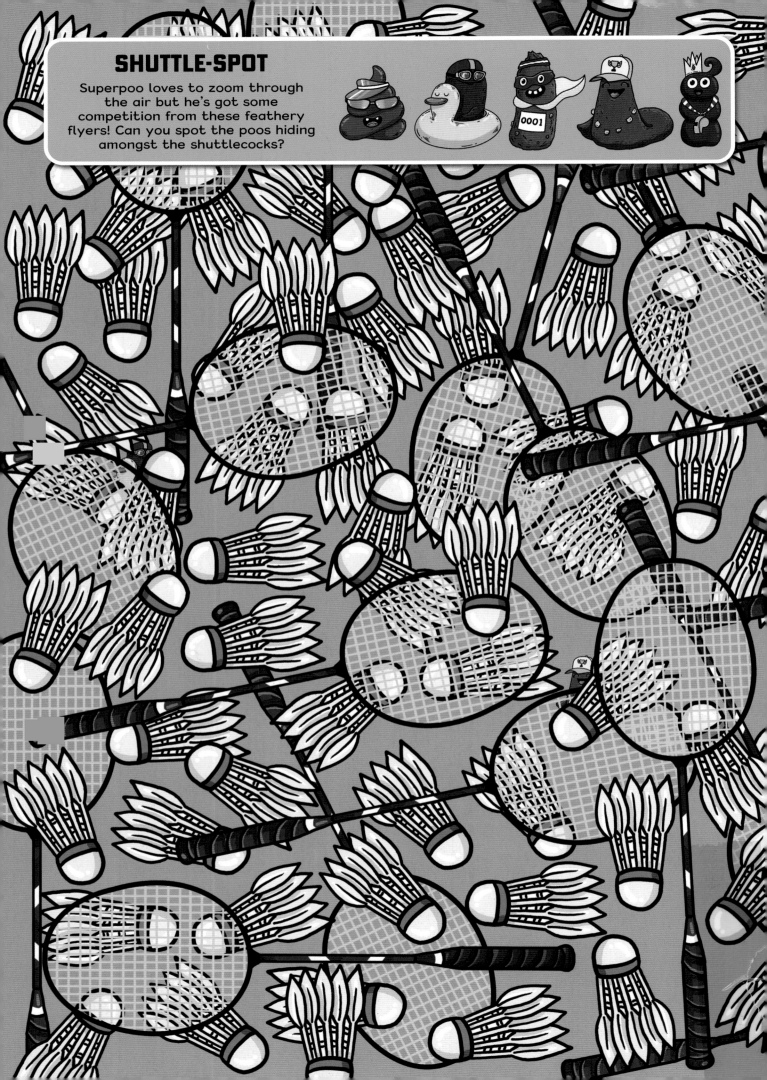

SHUTTLE-SPOT

Superpoo loves to zoom through the air but he's got some competition from these feathery flyers! Can you spot the poos hiding amongst the shuttlecocks?

ODD ONE OUT!

Which shuttlecock and racket are the odd ones out?

PENALTY POOP-OUT

The poos are cheering on their favourite team at the football match. Penalty to the reds! Can you find all the poos enjoying this beautiful game?

BALANCE BEAM BOBBI

The poos are in awe of the gymnasts vaulting and somersaulting. Watch you don't get trodden on, Bobbi!

0001

GO FOR GOLD

Elvis thinks there's nothing cooler than winning a gold for the team. Spot him and the poos eyeing up the prizes.

SKATE PARK SUPERSTAR

Don't underestimate Queenie on a skateboard – her backside flip is the best! Find all the poo friends showing off their tricks.

DUCKING AND DIVING

Duckie's in his element weaving down the rapids in his lightning-fast rubber ring. No one can keep up with him.

ANSWERS

Now try and find the extra items hidden in each scene.

POOLSIDE

5 stripy balls ☐

5 swimming noodles ☐

4 pairs of armbands ☐

5 doughnut inflatables ☐

3 cameras ☐

1 orange frisbee ☐

5 pairs of flippers ☐

3 water bottles ☐

1 inflatable fish ☐

1 pink spotted swimming cap ☐

VELO VROOM

2 bike pumps ☐

1 dog ☐

5 spanners ☐

7 spare wheels ☐

1 penny-farthing ☐

3 yellow helmets ☐

6 cartons of popcorn ☐

3 cardboard boxes ☐

A person with a head bandage ☐

6 cyclists with green helmets ☐

BALL BONANZA

PUTTING POOS

2 frogs ☐

3 yellow birds ☐

1 mouse ☐

7 flags ☐

3 butterflies ☐

3 buckets of golf balls ☐

1 kite ☐

1 banana ☐

2 dogs ☐

3 people in red hats ☐

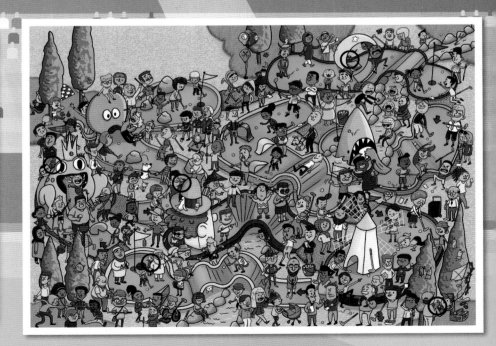

ON YOUR MARKS

- 5 video cameras ☐
- 1 dog mascot costume ☐
- 9 javelins ☐
- A high-jumper ☐
- A man in a green tie ☐
- 1 water bottle ☐
- 1 Union Jack flag ☐
- 3 discuses ☐
- 4 people with clipboards ☐
- 1 microphone ☐

STINKY WICKET

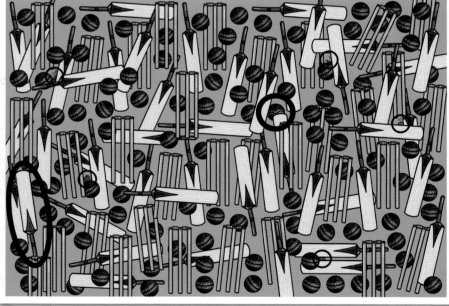

SPEED SEEKERS

4 white arrows ☐

18 traffic cones ☐

5 green flags ☐

10 orange helmets ☐

6 pink race cars ☐

14 people with moustaches ☐

A stack of 8 tyres ☐

1 trophy table ☐

A person waving a red flag ☐

2 people in yellow overalls ☐

IT'S SNOW JOKE

1 snowman ☐

2 birds ☐

4 green snowmobiles ☐

9 red flags ☐

1 cat ☐

1 abominable snowman ☐

1 snowplough ☐

4 ski lifts ☐

A man in a tree ☐

2 red sleds ☐

SHUTTLE-SPOT

PENALTY POOP-OUT

- 14 foam fingers ☐
- 8 white balls ☐
- 1 guide dog ☐
- 22 hot dogs ☐
- A footballer with green hair ☐
- 2 people carrying trays ☐
- 2 yellow flags ☐
- 1 whistle ☐
- 1 pair of yellow gloves ☐
- 2 blue hats ☐

BALANCE BEAM BOBBI

- 5 whistles ☐
- 11 water bottles ☐
- 2 gold medals ☐
- 5 wooden stools ☐
- 1 purple rucksack ☐
- 10 clipboards ☐
- 3 gold cups ☐
- 1 green leotard with stars on ☐
- 5 bouncy balls ☐
- 3 bananas ☐

GO FOR GOLD

Did you find me? If you're stuck, try visiting the gymnasium again.

SKATE PARK SUPERSTAR

5 pigeons ☐

2 cats ☐

3 purple skateboards ☐

A radio ☐

A painting of a rainbow ☐

A red bicycle ☐

7 scooters ☐

14 people falling over ☐

2 rucksacks ☐

3 skaters in matching outfits ☐

DUCKING AND DIVING

2 picnic blankets ☐

5 yellow dinghies ☐

3 dolphins ☐

38 fish ☐

2 babies ☐

2 people who've fallen in ☐

2 purple canoes ☐

2 people in red hats ☐

2 waterfalls ☐

A person in a red jumper ☐

ORCHARD BOOKS
First published in Great Britain in 2021 by The Watts Publishing Group © 2021 The Watts Publishing Group Limited
Illustrations by Dynamo Limited   Additional images © Shutterstock
A CIP catalogue record for this book is available from the British Library
ISBN 978 1 40836 499 4   Printed and bound in China   1 3 5 7 9 10 8 6 4 2

Orchard Books, an imprint of Hachette Children's Group
Part of The Watts Publishing Group Limited, Carmelite House, 50 Victoria Embankment, London, EC4Y 0DZ
An Hachette UK Company   www.hachette.co.uk   www.hachettechildrens.co.uk

MIX
Paper from responsible sources
FSC® C104740